Fairy Win

Bird Wings

Top Hat

Mirror

Asteroid

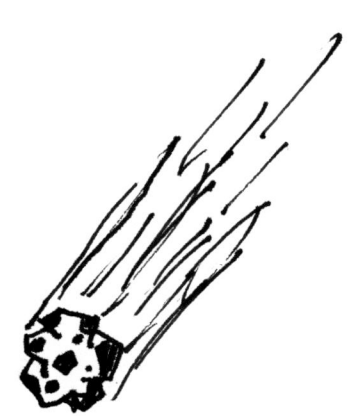

Earth

Book

Rose

Lotus Flower

---

key

Tree

Light Sword

Light Shield

Grim Reaper

Fountain

Goddess

Angel

lighting

Mask

Jackal

Deer

Bear

Medusa

Unicorn

Carousel

Tiki Idol

Voodoo Doll

Skull

Sugar Skull

Lamp

Camp Fire

Tooth

Robot

Totem Pole

Dream Catcher

Beach

Sunset

Wave

Zodiac Sign

Bunny

Snake

Computer

Lightbulb

Football

Hummingbird

Mammoth

T-Rex

Whishing Well

Pool

Target

Bouquet of Roses

Aurora Borealis

Radio

Television

phone

Movie ticket

Bowling pins

Banjo

Labyrinth

Kraken

Pegasus

Armadillo

Egg

cup

jack-in-the box

Zombie

vampire

Chalis

Shepher

Flag

Maze

Hook

Water Slide

necklase

Warrior

Pinata

Carrot

apple

Colosseum

bubble gum

soup

crystal ball

cheese

crystal

Rubber Ducky

Bath tub

Flamingo

Frog

Sword

Helmet

INK=Messy

Candle

tent

Hourglass

honeycomb

fire

---

compass

Stonehenge

Snow globe

teddy bear

car

rocking chair

Palm tree

Clock

Racetrack

Playing Cards

Jungle

lily pad

---

smile

eye

ear

hand

pants

. Spear

Sheriffs badge

gecko

samurai

Toy Robot

Nutcracker

Sundial

Tacos

hamburger

Milk carton

Dragon

Superhero

Arrow

Parrot

Cemetery

Atom

stain glass window

---

ghost

monkeys

bracelet

wand

sunflowers

mailbox

police

doctor

desk

orange

mango

butterfly

moth

snowflake

UFO

cloud

parachute

obelisk

tower

bridge

Frankenstein

test tube

---

roller coaster

skates

---

basket

bikini

pizza

kangaroo

---

tiger

ring

tablet

cyclops

minotaur

scissors

bed

elf

---

orc

ant

elemental horse

fish

magic broom

donut

pirate

cat

nurse

club

---

bomb

shovel

helicopter

treasure map

Eifel tower

row boat

---

owl

griffin

---

axe

pumpkin

toy soldier

water drop

pirate flag

tiara

sombrero

wizards hat

magic door

fire ball

flying car

fedora

···

pencil

ruler

crown

throne

---

maid

Made in the USA
Columbia, SC
21 December 2024